Green Point Bearings

Kathryn Fry

Green Point Bearings

For

family

and

friends

Green Point Bearings
ISBN 978 1 76041 512 9
Copyright © text Kathryn Fry 2018

First published 2018 by
GINNINDERRA PRESS
PO Box 3461 Port Adelaide 5015 Australia
www.ginninderrapress.com.au

Contents

Going One Way	7
Ferry to Bobbin Head	9
Under the Old Tangle	10
Green Point Bearings	12
Bottlebrush	16
So	17
Going One Way	18
Sandstone Country	20
On the Putty Road	21
Histories	23
Iningai Reserve	25
Water Myths	26
Desert Pea	30
HISTORIES	31
The Muddied Path	34
Tracing the Hours	35
If there's loss here, I'll never find it	37
Outlook	38
Art Talk	39
Chinese pots and lemons (1982)	41
Triptych	42
The Folly	44
Cows and Pulpit Rock	45
What I admire most about you, Margaret,	46
With Jacqueline du Pré	47
Art Talk	48
Greater than the Sum	49
Learning to Grieve	51

The Bowen Mango	52
After the News	53
Tending the Memory of Two Sisters	54
Motherlode	56
Soldier	59
All the Willing Hours	60
Kingfisher	61
Their Hands	62
Greater than the Sum	64
Year's End at the Goodradigbee	66

Here — 67

Awabakal	69
After the Office	70
The Bogey Hole	72
Here	73
Muogamarra	74
Notes from Barrington	75
A Simple Mix	76
Lunch in the Gardens	78
Sydney Rock Orchid	79
On Meeting a Colony	80
Solstice	81
Holding Firm	82

Notes	87
Acknowledgements	88

Going One Way

Ferry to Bobbin Head

                      History is falling
from Barrenjoey, whispering from the bays
of Refuge, Flint and Steel, and the smooth lips
of their beaches: Hungry, Resolute and Eleanor.

                      We're enclosed by contours
of memory in the sandstone carved to cliff and cave,
in the hill-folds' slow tumble to the stone-edged water,
and that tree, a bonsai on rock.

                      West Head sits in shadow and late
light as we ferry the Hawkesbury swell. And I recall when
we first set course on our voyage together, and ever since,
the crests and the calm.

Under the Old Tangle

No matter now who carried those seeds
across the seas from the prairie states,
from Red River valley, their lumbering trees

prized by the Osage tribesmen to strike
into bows. Such trees, their large globes
of sticky-sap fruit with a hint of citrus.

No matter now who stripped the land
to set the row for the boundary running
north–south, in time a line of overarching

limbs in grey. I bend below the lurch
of branches, thorny and leafless and rising
from this relic in the bowl of green hills

by the Hawkesbury. Wattle and bracken
blend with narrow leaf cottonbush in
the clearing of the black weathered breccia

of Peats Crater. The ramblers gather, some
walk to the creek in light rain. It's no matter
we'll have gone our single ways tomorrow.

Nature knows her reasons: curved low in
this hedge of Osage Orange and reaching
into the shaded earth, its wood loops

in the colour of clean, clear flame. It matters
how an image flickers then into my mind
of eyes holding the glow of their own orison,

the bright drive of their worth. Someone
who stands out in the thicket of others, who
answers to self and the seasons, who knows

the feel of my fingers. And under the old
tangle of timber, I think how I still love rolling
the syllables of his name around in my mouth.

Green Point Bearings

i To step in

Facing a long-slimmed trunk lit white among green
line and form, the leaves tapering and tough, their
trees are a cast of characters on this set. That fig
by the water's stage, spread for picnics under its limbs.

Green Point lures a crowd and chronicles its past
in notes by the track. How it took years, yes years
before this opened for the taking: a reserve
offering glints of blue between the columns

exhaling into the mix of moisture and sea salts,
a neighbourhood softer than the box and hide
of suburban brick, a semblance of the once-wild,
a remnant to step in, to seek from.

Now lorikeets hurtle through the curve of the hill,
the sea eagle rises above spotted gums (the vista
in his sweep). Fish spring above a cormorant's
chase, the lake rough with breaking eddies;

opposite, a gully goes out of sight covered
in tangle. Myrtle honey slips in on a breeze
and I think of the places we used to walk,
the words said in the company of gums.

ii A virtual midden

I'm taking Green Point bearings across
a lapse of time. A river valley becomes
a lake holding bark canoes, murmurings
of Awabakal. Over the centuries, spent
shells in the sandy gravel have rolled

into bleached bits by my feet. Once, by
a river, you said, 'Schubert is in the rapids.'
The world bright again. Below the lookout
on water blue as the sky's day, a quarry
gouged the millennia's conglomerate

smoothed now to parkland; a magpie pins
his lizard. You could read a land like this;
could sum its seasons in a scan. Salt
of the earth, you called yourself and many.
Nearby, a powerful owl rests in a mahogany.

Years-old timber toppled&turned to huts,
shingles and wharves, pit props and brigs
to ferry the Tasman (the *Kate Moynahan*,
the *Eliza Mary*). Today above the pier,
dollar birds cackle and hawk for flies,

a man casts for fish. Men in past mines
scoured the Great Northern and Fassifern
seams, their splint and cherry. Seventy-two
down Belmont's bord and pillar,
a Golden Egg in the lockout of '29.

I'm walking in a virtual midden
from Black Jack's to Hartley Point, reeling
in cadences of lost voices, letting your laughter
hive among these. And the way you'd throw out
your arms as if in gathering, you belong.

iii Even in wind

summoned from the south
or west, tingling leaves,
swishing fronds,
sashaying branches, tossing

butterflies, but not the bellbirds
pealing a melody in high E/F
in irregular time, tuning me to you,
elder-voice on my shoulder.

iv A legacy like yours

There was rain overnight, running from
the clay into frog holes and insect havens.
On the hill the canopy hums. Today there's
no smog in the south, nor smoke.

The birds are out, the sun angled so it wills them
at midday: pardalote and Lewin's honeyeater
jostling for airplay with whip and butcher birds,
even weebills in the high leaves singing

up the waning moon, the equinox just passed,
sensing the year's running. Here you'd stop
and breathe in the scene as if it were all
the manna you need. And so I know

Green Point is a sanctuary of soil and sound
and light slanting on gum tips and bracken,
the shimmer on water and wing, a mirror
on the calm of silence and stillness.

The sun's rays on clumps under the lake's skin
– the greens and pinks for seahorses, sea hares
and fish – from here, at the top of the cliff-face
among a wide-girthed stand too high for logging,

a legacy like yours, this gift in the common good
of littoral forest. Ripples come clear to the foreshore
pebbles and wrack; the pocket rainforest closes
on a flowing creek, paperbarks and low ferns.

Note: splint and cherry refers to the alternating types of coal: coarse, dull, hard coal (splint) and a soft, black, caking coal (cherry).

Bottlebrush

Callistemom citrinus

Each bud sets a slow stretch
above the petals. The red, a flare
of filaments and style for the bee
and honeyeater, at night the glider.

Nectar the reward, pollen the prize
– the half-prize – swelling ovules
to seeds to drift as specks on the soil:
sandy, clayey, in shade or not.

The shoot becomes a shrub
with lemon in the rub of its leaves.
And in the lengthening light past
winter, red tips emerge…

So

If you like the flash and set of flowers
up against each other in stippled light
on a sandstone rise, the track a multicolour
of leaves or quartz-white sand on a ridge;

if you like to hike a hundred metres above
the water lines at Naa Badu Lookout where
the creeks join, and look down between
trees and the wedge peas' eyes of sun;

if you like to listen for the pardalote,
whip bird, and the silence of a fragile marsh,
and to stride the hills from Crosslands to Cowan,
hearing yellow-taileds above the boronias,

come then…

Going One Way

i

Among the riches of the Lane Cove River,
its shaded shrubs, its wet-weather falls,
a place for breathing long and deep;
and flannel flowers holding what winter
light they can and bringing you

to my thoughts. And in the Berowra Valley,
lobelias rise from fire-grit, blue in their hair-fine
greenery. This country is a sandstone song
swelling now with boronias' pink
under angophoras and gums.

It shows me a fern I've never seen before
how the creek widens here (its ancient sands,
its stone-crush of ochre at the edge), adds
rapids there, how cocooned it all is from
the sky. In my mind I show you.

Grasstrees crown the slopes with patience
and the track brings a treecreeper, a party
of wrens, a pair of yellow robins. They sing
the score these waters write from sky
to sea. All day I walk, my bones singing us.

ii

It's the music of you I walk with. In August
wedding bush is white brilliance and lace,
eriostemons could be bridesmaids though
their champagne-pink is everywhere. Red
grevilleas are fists-full of hope, as winter

slips its grip. Descending to Galston Gorge
at noon, I'm in mid-air, and see us,
you and I, in midlife's heat and peace.
Isopogons near a sun orchid, mat rush
by the track, pea plants in bud – as if

I see more knowing you. Later
near Crosslands with the tide ebbing,
yellow-tailed are high above, their black
wings long and lazy in the thin light,
the two of them heading together.

Sandstone Country

After the hundred-year drought, water falls like
we've never seen, throws cloud to chill the lungs.

Winter sun slants at trees. You spot palms
hundreds of metres down.

What is it about this place?

You stop me by lichens crowding what's left of a trunk.
I show you the honey flower, spidery club moss and cornstalks.

You steady a banksia and we stare down the tube,
its massed pins like starburst.

I point out the rush of white-water to the falls and you say
I've caught the infinity pool.

You question the time taken to carve its creek into the valley,
so much to contemplate

like the spaces between us before the walk and how
suddenly they've disappeared.

Everything here speaks of infinity.

On the Putty Road

Fusion of green around the gleam
of new bark on *grandis* & *saligna*
& the sunburst of
wattle-glow
on the Putty Road, its narrow turns
between
Yengo & Wollemi,
hills steeped in a mass
of thin limbs among old stone.

Off the road to a fireplace
under a sandpaper fig, the scene fills
with sound: a guide full
of frogs & birds, surviving
on the changes in leaves & sap
& cambium, the chemistry
that begins & ends with light,
the mystery ongoing,
the mastery going on.

Histories

Iningai Reserve

Gidgees cut for fuel, goats kept for meat
or milk; the Longreach Common cracked deep
and bare. Some sixty years on, the goats

have gone, the Iningai long before. But bones
interred in the Keeping Place are singing up
the downs, those curly and bull, barley and hoop

that billow and yellow the Mitchell grasslands
and spread a damp-blade sweetness for the whistlers,
the lofty kingfisher, the roos at rest, those two

brolgas rising, the kites' nests by Gin Creek.
Elders singing up the commune of leaves:
the mulga and myall, bootlace oak and gum,

wild orange and bush bauhinia shading
the clay; spirits free again to read the shifting
stars or just now, singing up the swelling clouds.

Water Myths

i

Women on plastic chairs shift in the sand
as the scientist lifts the box to their table.
Mungo Lady brought back, safe in country;
a breeze rustles her spirit home.

They spread her cracked, charred bones
on the velvet lining and cry the same tears
of forty thousand years before – and this,
the first cremation for our world to know.

'She's not your ancestor,' the archaeologist said.
'We've always been here,' they said. 'She surfaced
for a reason. If you find something, bury it deeper.'
They found Mungo Man, arthritis in his bones.

But right here, right now, the wind cuts
to my core, carves down the lunette it once
shaped from fossil lakes after the old Lachlan
and Willandra Creek and the plenty ended.

The ranger crouches by an ancient fireplace,
tells of shellfish middens and golden perch
near a shingleback sleeping by the track, emus
out there and somewhere a singing honeyeater.

ii

In 1861
near the rugged stone in Mutawintji Gorge
Ludwig Becker sat certain as the spindly cypress.
His pen in sepia ink, he sketched the rocks
(where thousands met in thousands of years)
and the pool then deep and clear in its bed.
Some touchstone to hold onto
in his final months on the long trek north.

Here now, we see the stencils he noted:
prints in red, yellow and white, all sizes,
left hands. Beyond the cooking pits
in the Historic Site, chiselled into slabs
of dry rock: old story surfacing in camps
and tracks, an emu, a ceremonial headdress.
Around them, mulga and dead finish acacias
hanging on.

iii

There are no limits on the road to
Pooncarie, out with the pearl bluebush
in the spread of land that flows all the way
to greet the sky like some vast ocean of soul.

And Menindee's dry for Broken Hill, too far
south for summer rain, too far north for winter's.
Nine lakes empty. How life aches and asks,
how much liquid lies under for the bores?

Towns blame one another for water loss.
Someone curses the drought and someone
the Authority and someone the crops way north.
By the unsealed road, all the lambs are twins.

Mallee trunks lean about in the bulldust. And clover
floods the waterless basin of the Great Anabranch.
Across the Darling, black cormorants peg boughs,
their throats silent over the river's wan run.

On the veranda of the old homestead
our guide bends for his boots; we amble
around the drop-log quarters and sheds
as he brings the past forward.

Thirty hands once on this station, campers and over-
night rooms now. His city memories crowd
the walls of wood panels in the breakfast room.
'Out there,' she points to the floodplain,

'when the muso settled his sax at our concert's end,
you should have heard the birds begin.'
Country has become them both
as if they've known it all their lives.

And us.
She gathers oranges in morning frost,
fills the jug to toast the sun in the river red gums
in their paradise.

Desert Pea

Swainsona formosa

There, above the gibbers and crusty
earth, the rise of red on a wash
of green – red flags, red keels, the dark
lustrous boss in between, ready,
florid David among the arid Goliath.

I'll grow you here, in the newly parched,
to course rampant down my brick
walls, to carry the cool stars of a desert
night, the light swamping a red-ochre range,
and the optimism you ride, on a whiff of rain.

HISTORIES

i Defined
after *Terra Spiritus...with a darker shade of pale* (1993–1998)
by Bea Maddock (1934–2016)

Two centuries past the voyage around,
she charts from map to graph to sheet
a fine wash outlining the island's
shoreline cliffs and inner hills.

Fifty pages soft-circle the gallery
walls with ochre she found and fixed
smooth to paper in a dozen tones.
And there in her dark and ferric sea

two cultures in counterpoint: one
courts the eye so I mouth its script:
lineneloomma, *lowwontumemeter*,
kribbiggerrer...how the names roll

and run full-bellied in the plane,
the Palawa decisive in her cursive,
each frame speaks bodily of loss,
each a murmur of history's wrath.

Below are labels typeset like bits
of metal shackled in the depths.
We know them still: Cape Grim
Oyster Cove, Flinders Island...

ii In the Shed

His smile is all heart.
song in Dalabon,
lips lined with supple
with old bush recall.

rubbed with red ochre
in paperbark, his aunt
to teach always
'Sometime no tucker

our culture dies'.
the white cockatoo
froth, his beard
us to cross-hatch

We follow him out
his eyes every which
in and back as if
his hand all pride

He sings a going away
his tongue and open
sounds, eyes warm
Born in Arnhem Land

and roo blood, wrapped
ever at him 'to learn
to never break the law'.
at night, only water…

On the didge he blows
dance, his hair a black
salty-grey. He teaches
with a wisp of reed.

to hunt the tin roo
way, his legs folding
they're spear-ready,
his smile all heart.

iii In the Sand

                          I can tell you
only how her eyes hold the whole Ipolera
above her faded shirt, how her hands circle
her story and her feet take a dusting
of fine, red sand as she walks;

how there's a bounty of flowering about
the boulders. She talks the business she gives
her Arrernte girls. In Tjilpa land, we women wait
near mistletoe, wild tobacco and colour
that comes from rain.

She speaks of the stars of the Southern Cross,
of Hermannsburg and searching the Finke.
She sketches wide custodial curves of story
to take beyond the baked sandstone
and the spinifex and silver-leaf.

The Muddied Path

Crisp cracks at birdcall, chainsaw
and the rewind of a mechanical shutter;
the lyrebird whips and whirls close by.
Our children collect stones.

Gums give way to floored trunks
covered in moss, thick enough to hide
your hand; more moss by the creek
on boulders, the air water-heavy.

Chartreuse and char-grey. To know
the way light enlivens texture, with you
summing up the rocks and soil, narrating
the eras. Or to linger, to let this world

inside. Right now the children scamper.
Soon they'll be hungry,
                    their lungs full of mountain air.
Already the little one is asleep on your back.

Tracing the Hours

i

Bird calls thick as stars above the King Edward
and finches rising in a whirring cloud by my feet
then breakfast of spice damper. A simple dough

baked medium hot like the day to come,
when we'll walk over sandstone, under fan palms
and by cocky apple on the Mitchell Plateau.

Our guide fills his bottle from murky holes,
finds wallabies for his children to chase, barefoot
and happy, out of school, learning Wandjina stories.

The boy tells us one, then climbs a bush plum,
legs straddling the branches, jiggling up and down.
The teenager collects fruit we don't eat.

You should hear them playing at crocodiles
in the water, though no one's in the spirit pool.
The youngest comes with us in the helicopter.

Back at base, they're all eyes: 'See any crocs?'
But it's the spread of mudflats that caught my eye,
that and the map line of coast and sea.

ii

Going south by the sprawl and triumph of white
lilies into forests in mist and their October flush,

we stand beneath the tingle and karri,
heaven-high water carriers of time;

and at Peaceful Bay where forest greets
the Great Southern Ocean, we're at ease

among the singing splendid wrens,
the knots of our long-term ties pulled smooth.

If there's loss here, I'll never find it

Nor can I know
when the fruit dove or the leech
first found themselves in rainforest time

or when the pink leaves of this red cedar
stretched through the canopy
fifty metres above, limiting light

but not birdsong and the air
cooling my skin under the tips
of ferns nestled up the trunks.

Over the relic of hot rock
on Dorrigo Mountain, water falls
from the sky, sudden as found bliss.

Outlook

I'm beside you, sharp-eyed for jutting
rocks and cars careering round the bends.

We pull over into Hanging Mountain Lookout.
It's easier to accept loss here, with the silence,
fuchias in two-tones, and the arcs of grass trees
reddening in the low rays of the winter sun.

You're feeling old, you say. By the fire tower,
mountains bulky and bold with being, stretch
around us, each range a blue paler than the next.
The peak you climbed once, faint atop the last.

We breathe the unbounded and the ageless,
this homecoming.

Art Talk

Chinese pots and lemons (1982)

'Flowers in vases and fruit: that's all there is to them.'
Margaret Olley (1923–2011)

I cannot know how an artist thinks.
Here's flourish and glint, a meditation
more teal than tea-green, more mint
than myrtle, more jade than celadon.

Nor have I known two deaths as those
that year: her mother Grace, lover
Sam. How she reached to hold close
her palette, her blank board.

How she placed. How she brushed
russet, umber and a little sienna
into the effort of bench, background
and woven wicker, and what was not.

How she spaced curve and lip, belly
and thin handle, ridge, neck and sure
base, gold-hip and glaze, lemon-leaf,
wisp and flowers, ripe before the fall.

Triptych

i White

after Rosemary Laing's photograph *flight research #5* 1999

We see you above the path of birds, above
the mountain range bordering a sapphire sky.

We see you above the lace of cloud, your arms
in immaculate white above the cumulus of your skirt.

And when it happens, we women of the world
will band together and bend to break your fall.

ii Blue

after William Robinson's *Bright Sea at Cape Byron, 2007*

There's the toss and swell of blue in the bay,
and foliage greening under every last lick of light.

There's the rim of ultramarine by the foreshore,
the daily murmurs and the silence laid on linen.

I step in and run under the opaline sky,
the wind cool on my chest.

iii Yellow

after Fred Williams's *Landscape 74*

This gorge, its staccato scrub to breathe here on canvas,
tone next to half-tone. He swirls the rocks, floats

the foreground by a hint of water. The intervals
between trees draw him in their light. And yellow to glaze

one day on a wall, to beckon song birds in the cycling
of seasons and the smell of bush grass after rain.

The Folly

After Fiona Hall's *Folly for Mrs Macquarie*,
The Royal Botanic Garden, Sydney

Melody flows out through the calm of interlaced iron, a cage of heart-curves and barbed arches and lines of pine needles. The aria glides wordless around the wideness of the Moreton Bay figs with their green fruit dangling, down past the grey miner foraging in the high red of a Gymea lily, past grevilleas and wrens in the rockery, down into the harbour's shimmer and glint and across to Mrs Macquarie's Chair. A Chinese man in midnight-blue makes music in the early light. He sits with his two-stringed fiddle on a block of cut sandstone and draws slow notes to swirl in the shelter about him, into the airy ceiling with bits of bone soldered to bone. He bows an absence of dissonance to the daggered hand at the top and the axe over the entrance poised never to strike. A younger man, unhurried on the grass, takes off his shirt and leans into the windless morning, surrounded as we all are in the drift from this hive of story, its past swelling in tune with the mild midwinter now.

Cows and Pulpit Rock

Arthur Boyd, 1998

One cow dog-alert, the other
easy in her bones, the foreground
a wash of summer yellow.

Brushmarks above the river:
ferns and rock orchids in the gullies,
wildflowers and gums below

his cerulean sky. He reveals
his caged heart from war dreams
and early bible:

the bride, the chains, Nebuchadnezzar,
the tortured lovers, what we have become
or could. Our hearts chilled,

we cross the river flats in silence.
No boats on the Shoalhaven, no wind,
though the parrots are restless.

What I admire most about you, Margaret,

not your eye for colour and light
nor your skill, the pigments and brush,
not your love of flowers and lustrous shapes
nor your party-girl whimsy
your dead-set lines, that originality,
your knocking convention
your philanthropy, far-reaching.

No, what I admire most, Margaret,
is how you let art grip you, right
to the moment of your last breath,
paint clinging to your fingers.

With Jacqueline du Pré

Elgar's Cello Concerto in E minor, Opus 85

She draws chords for an ocean at dawn,
>   a wavering along the shoreline,
>   a tarry on the sand.
Elgar's lament on the Great War, wordless
>   on this cloudless morning by the sea.

Her body the soundboard.
>   We hear *the loss,*
>   *the loss, an ocean of loss*.
Her left fingers like bees at their source;
>   her right hand curved to a swan's head.

She leans like a lover to her cello, leans away,
>   leads us to a field. And the rose swells
>   in double delight, fading to white at the centre.
She has his music by heart, knows how to be
>   half-way through life.

From her mother's score and sketch by her pillow,
>   fresh melodies skilled to sway the child
>   and walks to the tones of forest and sea.
Now his final movement, the swagger and bustle,
>   all on stage pitching in.

She's fiery, hair tossed back,
>   fills us with ache.
>   She too has gone, lost
like them too soon
>   and yet, we say, never.

Art Talk

Once we shared all the moments in a day.
Our city defined then by the river's brown
amble through the suburbs, houses peeling
in the sun. We stood on the edge tossing out
questions; all heat, hormones and hope.

Years on, our worlds separate, our worldly
concerns the same. We meet in the gallery
before the artist's clean lines, his mirrors
to hushed cities, oil drums and trucks,
lone figures and a smart self-portrait.

Precision in his paint opens the sky,
carries us into an easy air, sieves
the years, lengthens this hour, lifts us
it seems, to the peak of a mountain above
the colours, with no need for questions.

Greater than the Sum

Learning to Grieve

i.m. Gaynor England

Now when I look at sweet peas in bloom
I remember how you had them in a row
below the water tank, wanting and
waiting for the flowering.

Now when I look at sweet peas,
I remember the yellow box by the dry
creek, the farm dogs scampering, how
you spoke about the years we hadn't shared,
how you worked to mend broken links.

Did you know then, when we wandered
in your garden, our eyes meeting above
the thick-leafed, tight-growing green
that I would see and you would not?

The Bowen Mango

for Jean Kent

One of us always plucked the seed
from the chopping board after our mother
skinned and sliced the mango and loaded
its flesh into her crystal bowl with other
tropical succulence, enough colour for all
of us. She'd be at the kitchen sink when

whoever scooped the prize carried it out
through the breakfast room with its wall
of small glass squares looking west into
Brisbane leaves and light, down the green
steps past the cluster of pawpaw trees grown
from tossed seed, to lean over the heap

of garden clippings in the yard, where I see
my older brother, who later enlisted to fight
in Vietnam. How he turned to me that day,
the seed's fibres sucked stiff near his lips,
his grin all larrikin, even with the trail of juice
trickling down the length of his arm.

After the News

She lies on her bed, hands
clenched, her face buried,
legs scissoring the covers.

Someone says the good go young.
Someone gives a cake.
Someone says he's gone to God.

red eyes raw eyes
        howling
                bury the moon

Later, making porridge for the youngest, she leans
against the stove, her gown undone,
her tears dropping into the mix.

Before action in Vietnam, her eldest
at twenty-one, is dead. The coffin lowers,
the soil shifts into her heart.

Tending the Memory of Two Sisters

i

The whorls of petals, pearl-white, beckon
– a curve here, a fullness there, one
part-hidden, a layer reaching – like her stories:

Land Army Girls, rations for petrol, oranges
and sugar, sewing shirts, knitting socks for war,
the unravelling of '45.

In her teens as steady home help, she missed a career.

She married, had sons, weathered uphill
days of shearing, harvest and fires, drawing
solace from Church and town.

She travelled to us and we to her by inland hills lit
with Salvation Jane, her mothering arms open,
her hands folding our moments.

The rose we tend in memory of her is long-stemmed
and fragrant, though she wasn't tall
                                and seldom wore scent.

ii

Two cats in the doorway, one
cleans the other. Velvet drapes,
leather chairs, Bach in the room.

She spins, weaves and knits,
fashions bears from sheepskins –
a character for each new kin.

She resigned to turn their
bedridden father every few
hours, over six years.

She shows me a gown for
an unknown bride (the light
fall of her fine-wool crochet),

and her table mats, her tatting
of fractals. 'I have permission
to die,' she jests, 'now I've finished

your eight.' The cats settle,
one curls into her lap.
She gives us feijoas, our car full

of heady scent for the trip home.
The tree we grow to honour her
has yet to bear such fruit.

Motherlode

i Resolve

At 1 a.m., she's shouting, 'I'm getting outta here.
Where's my purse?' I turn on a light, and she's
clasping the purse in her hand. Oh, the clash
and jangle of her groans. She calls me my sister's

name; I hear the hell-bent wheeling of her mind.
Come morning she'll pop her blister pack of pills
and swallow all seven. And swear, 'These tablets,
they're keeping me…'   In my mother's wilderness,

oh God. Her drive (her old glue, the reasons she tired
and tires) has left her, not wholly bereft. She digs
deep for a memory, finds the weight of her father's
hand light on her arm, shows me his soothing strokes.

We settle to a hush and watch *The Dam Busters*
at noon (planes droning above the water,
the darkened grey easy on her blown maculae),
she's certain now about getting this war won.

The day I am to leave, she wills her hands
to the calm of her lap, her brow brushed clear
with resolve from her mothering well, the years
she had to give. And I know what she doesn't say.

There, as if she's where she always was.

ii The End Room

No complaints. None about the hospital soup,
the beef stew and corn, the apple crumble –
each time her mouth open like a hungry bird,

restraint aside, bled out on the ruptures
in her brain. 'Tell me, have I had a good life?'
Yes. We told her. She said 'Umm' at intervals,

her eyes expecting some unveiling. Born at home,
midnight, her dad racing for the doctor; ninety
plus summers; great-grand-children, names

like leaves on a tree; sixty-three years a wife,
a pen-pal for sixty; cuttings from the garden
to gladden the rooms; humming in the kitchen;

wanting a real job (the feel and flow of fabric);
moving with the thrill of sport, even the reruns.
'I'm so tired, so tired yet I can't sleep…'

No mention of those other traits knitted in us:
distance, a tendency to say no, that unfailing rivalry.

Her breathing constant till noon Tuesday, as tiny
beads formed on the yellowing of her upper lip
– her breaths like the flame of an old spirit lamp

then one final quiver we held her through.

iii There She Is

I'm looking for penguins in limestone holes
below the heath – gums, geebungs, grasses
picture-perfect in the salty wind – the waning
moon setting. Out of nowhere a fantail turns
and twists his feathers. And there she is,

walking as ever down the hall, her cool cotton
dress (floral waist-band and hem); hair fluffed,
face powder-fresh after every afternoon shower.
But here I've upset these masked lapwings
into a cackle of code over Nepean Bay.

Hers were Tiffany's dreams at breakfast,
a catwalk on Fifth Avenue, the fall of crepe,
the cut of linen, always the choice of colour.

She'd be the purple crowned lorikeet, flighty,
bright as every crayon in the pack, chalking up
the crimson of these flashy myrtle flowers.
But give her strelitzia's gold or gerberas, bowls
of pink magnolias, camellias large as plates.

Alone in those final years, she broke bread
for the butcherbird at her kitchen window.

'A long time gone,' you said. But I find you
in my sister's voice, my thinning hands
and now even where you've never been.

Soldier

She wanted her father to teach her fishing
or the woodwork he talked of turning to.

She bought him books and tools to get him
started. She dreamt they'd chat long and free

over lines in the river or choosing slabs
of sassafras or cedar. Lately she recalls

his last words to her. 'Take it easy.'
She almost didn't hear them.

Now she sees how he lived to the end:
she never guessed his battles,

the replays and recurrent flashes of war,
never guessed being could be so difficult,

never guessed he went fishing without
the lines, turned wood without the lathe.

All the Willing Hours

'& we shall walk & talk in gardens all misty with rain
& never never grow so old again'
Inscription, Wendy Whiteley's Garden, Sydney

Narrow paths centre the terraces through
fig and flame and bangalow palm; leaves jostle

the storeys with shape and shade and tint
any leaf will take. A sanctuary with roots

in her childhood; Lavender Bay her own
rampant alchemy to wander in, like a painting.

And for us too, picnic tables, a bell hanging
in meditation, a birdbath from a cast-out sink.

With her hair wrapped in folds of iris-blue,
Wendy tells how she replaced the debris among

the coral trees, cutting by cutting, plant
by plant and mulch, to revere them here:

her lover, their daughter. How all the willing
hours bloom unexpected grace from loss.

Kingfisher

for Deb Westbury

i

She's reading, her ear tuned for music
and the elusive metaphor, her hand
taking the pencil to the margin.

Rhododendrons light the drive
outside and the flowering peach flags
new leaves. Pied butcherbirds coo
to each other, one on a low branch,
the other encircling from tree to tree.

ii

This is the week the native iris unfolds
and wind unfurls more yellow.

Now, in mist over Jamison Valley,
Mt Solitary shoulders the early sun.
Cockatoos are specks of paper tracing
a silent path. Trees bunker in the depths,
shrubs hang from the cliff-face,
their backs to the warming stone.
Two scrub wrens come close,
nimble in their niche.

I read from her card:
'By the river I saw an azure kingfisher
snaffle a dragonfly in mid-air.
I thought I even heard the crunch.'

Their Hands

i

In the laundry, an old tin half-filled
with soap bits. We bring chocolates,
Pa places them in the buffet for next
winter. The meal is quick and quiet;
they smile at our children's chatter.

In the long evening we wander among
their garden of roses and fuchsias
and goldfinches at their bath.
We're in their world
as if they're my grandparents.

ii

There's birdsong before sunrise
and native shrubs with the weight of buds;
mountains jagged to the east. I wonder
if they know this mix of native scrub.
'You can have too many books,' Nan said.
They tolerate my late breakfast, out-of-routine.

iii

We visit Nan's school, their church and hall,
see the shape of their years in farming,
their paddocks edged by old, ragged pines.

The shed yields its heavy-heady mix
of dung and lanolin. Summer was fire
season, always fire season.

We stop by the home of her birth.
Beside the front door, two stained-glass
magpies look over yellowed pasture.

iv

I am now their age when we first met.
Yet what moves me more is the image
of their hands soft-stroking my children's hair.

Greater than the Sum

i

Risen in the unfurled whorls of cycads, in
grasses and sand-palms, in Darwin woollybutt
and ironwood after the burning – enough
green for a lifetime it seems.

And when I hold this light length of a bloom
near Florence Falls, its honey-scent summering
here in spring, I think of you in the fiery decline
of your health. Others check the heights

of cathedral mounds as if they're lost
to the industry inside, the pooling of chemicals
in clever chambers. It was you who held space
for me then, some sanctity I waded in.

At Ubirr I'm drawn to the ochre of a barramundi
on rock, and the sunset over the plains. A lightness
comes in this vastness

                and there you surface again.

ii

Buff-coloured birds, iron bleached from sand,
spindly shadows. I can't contemplate the heat
of high summer here. But I'd will you this –

a swim at Edith Falls under the tawny wings
of bee-eaters over and back, over and back
to grevilleas frilled in orange on the bank.

iii

An artist might catch the multi-petals of pink lotus
and the emerald plates for the Jesus bird to step to

on the billabong, or the leaves like bowls
begging in the sun. But if you could see the jabiru

turn his blue-shimmering neck or that pair
of brolgas fly over; if you could spot the cobalt

of the kingfisher as he darts and how he spins
from the surface without stopping…

iv

My hope for you here, in the surest of hours.
The land below is a page set in biota and earth

colours scripted over eons: islands of stone in seas
of woodland, the darkest code nestled in chasms.

The East Alligator River uncurls its silk all the way
to the Gulf of the Timor Sea where in 1845 by lagoons

'crowded with ducks and geese', Ludwig Leichhardt
found 'the stoutest and fattest men'.

Year's End at the Goodradigbee

Mile after mile of scorched trunks. We chat along
the dirt road, 'What will become of the mountain ash?'

Franklin's Hut, gone since the fire, its tank-stand a twisted
chair frame. Broad leaves crown the base of burnt trees.

Flowers sweep up the mountain. We pick our way through
grasses, clumps of colour and starworts everywhere.

You say, 'Since '36, we'd push our vehicles over the snow;
ski down, then catch the rope from John's ute.'

By the river south in slow time along this valley, past campers
and where Miles lived, her house no longer on that knoll.

'The airstrip was there, now who had that old pisé house;
oh, so good to ride home through this stretch, my horse knew;
Once it leaves the valley, it's a different river.'

At First Point in the low, cool water, a wren checks quickly,
a little sediment rises between filaments and bedded rock.

Here

Awabakal

Flowers coming out
as if it's their last chance.

Crammed and tough-leafed
among wattle and pea yellows
tea tree and myrtle whites
reds, mauves and blues
as if colours breathe life.
At the bluff, in starch-white sand

flannel flowers face the sea
in a flourish of exclamation marks.

After the Office

i Making Sushi

Out of the office, he sampled Han Sushi,
the lunch fresh, the colours squared
tight and clean in rice trimmed black.

Now retired, he's practised aligning
and rolling, the pressure just right
for the section's end-of-year today.

He thinks they'll relish the mix
of textures, that tang of vinegar, burst
of wasabi, nori rich from the sea.

He's going back to laughter, skilled
word games, thoughtful company.
They were such days, his final team

bright as a gift. Hot rice rests
on the bamboo mat, the long cuts
of red, green and orange line their bowls.

ii Finding Form

He recalls the meetings, emails,
the piles of paper, the proofs,
deadlines, last minute frenzies,
the published reports.

Now he tends his garden daily
seeking complexity in simple leaves.
He pictures individual cells, their fluid
full of molecules, their thick fibre walls

wrapped paper-thin. He collects
spring and summer greens and reds.
It's like biting into sweetness,
the thin and soft between his teeth.

The Bogey Hole

Hewn from rock under Shepherd's Hill, under a dutiful eye. Lashes for transgressions, cat-o'-nine-tails on each back to keep the convicts bound to Commander Morisset's bidding for a bath; a salty hole in the conglomerate-sandstone shelf. Named for ablutions and something of a menace. Over two centuries, day after night, water cycles through the pool, seeps into crevices at the pull of the moon and the choreography of clouds. Below me, a line of ten bare-chested teenagers between the posts, face east and wait for the seventh wave to skittle them silly, to whitewash each into a breathless ball, slip them over and pound them down among the living holdfasts. It's not the time to step into this pond, it's no jewel now on a finger of land, it's not the time to wade into the green-blue honeycombed with light. And it's not that time in late summer when you and I floated in the calm and clarity of each other.

Here

If I could paint you a scene, should it be

the moment of this lake – water calm and taut
as skin, fishermen on the jetty, mountains
in the far blue and birds about the morning?

Or this, as if caught in a clear bowl –

pipefish and leatherjacket, the tiny beating
wings of seahorses, some squid and shells
and shrimp, all young in the salty eelgrass?

or will I paint someone walking

over the blackened trunk and coal-dark branches
laid ages, ages ago beside the sea, now with pinks,
ambers and lilacs scattered in pebbles on the sand?

Or picture a swimmer, in the silk and glide
of the sea, spray hurling above oystercatchers
and silver gulls below the cliff top?

Far better that I have you with me, here.

Muogamarra

I search for a native rose:
the scent of her magenta buds,
the delicate leaves tugging at stems.

You find a whale engraved in sandstone.
Nearby are heaths, their stalks burnished white,
and an island with moss around a single shrub.

We talk of a lone spore falling on a rock,
run a time-lapse through the mind:
the slow-arrowed pace of this place.

On a ridge in Muogamarra
in a sphere of wax flowers, peas and boronias,
I scan the poise of their single shapes.

I'm always looking for something somewhere else,
but when you show me what you've found, my eyes
settle on the sure stance of you.

Notes from Barrington

We ride the unsealed road twisting
the long way to the falls, wade the rock-strewn
river, cows and calves stilled as we pass.
We study the thousand metre drop,
the collage canopy, ridgelines that span down
like fingers, hills clasping their valleys.

We stop under Antarctic beech, relics
leaf-dot a grey sky and tower over fiddleheads
and moss on the edge of the escarpment.
We walk by pepperbush and snow grass,
the wind unexpectedly cold and icy with moisture
cleansing chest and throat.

An age-old orchestra in the lie of this land
plays adagio andante allegro appassionato.

Over the tangle of waterlogged channels
two flame robins skim above tassel sedge,
crimson rosellas chatter and forage
in hollows of snow gum and black sallee.

A Simple Mix

Slivers of rosemary and sage release
tangs of pine and lemon as she cuts.

She adds spinach, crisp with last night's rain,
zucchinis, their flesh a gradient of green.

She cracks the eggs, foams the whites,
creams yolks with a long pour of extra

virgin olive oil and shavings of parmesan,
ripe and dry as a midday in summer,

into which she folds flour, sifted air-light.
On the leaf-flecked mixture in the dish,

she places grape tomatoes just gathered
from the garden, spacing the halves

in symmetry as if to pattern the success
their long living brings to her.

Over each oval fruit, a holdfast of thyme
like the weave of their being together.

A simple mix, yet its scents catch
in her an ease, as the breath

of a desert in bloom or such places
they'll discuss through the afternoon,

or current affairs, theirs and the world's
from their decades, the art

that moves them still. Oven aromas spiral
as she carries bread to the table.

She greets them both at the door,
the sun on her face.

Lunch in the Gardens

Two elderly sisters, same height
and white hair, sit by the bromeliads.
One's skirt is pale as the other's blue
hat. They unwrap lunch on the bench.

Behind them, a butcherbird pins
a mouse on a tree limb; he pecks
grey fur, tries a snip, then lugs it
along the branch. It slips and drops.

He dives to the leaf litter; the women look
into the purple blades, eating wordlessly.
The bird hauls his prey up. It falls.
He heaves it high. Again and again.

He drags it, his eyes hard at their rims.
He grips his claws into the bundle
and flies. The sisters rise,
crumbs scatter like spent souls.

Sydney Rock Orchid

Dendrobium speciosum

Behind the statue of a boy extracting
a thorn (all in smooth white marble),
I find you among ferns, but your scent spills
even from the nearly-spent cascades.

Near succulents too in the gardens
you landscape rock in today's shade,
a riot of disorder and the haphazard.
Your flourish of leaves plumped thick

under the last arches of blooms, each
with so many altars for bees and eyes
to land on and wander among the cream
curves and cloisters, settling time.

And when the pods harden and shed,
a zillion seeds will dust up the wind, away
from the concrete, glass and bitumen;
a few will drop into damp, dark crevices.

Any crop of sandstone is suspect now.
I'll be out and back, watching for new canes,
their erupting stems and swellings. All year
I'll wait for the gathering of seasonal grace.

On Meeting a Colony

Elodina angulipennis

A hundred light wings
ruffle the air,

wander and quiver
and interweave.

Dusk-tipped pearls.
Moonsails pulse

around and between two
native pomegranate trees.

My mind eases
out of itself

to drift with the billowing
tremulous white.

Solstice

On a stout limb of an ironbark
two wood ducks call and rouse
each other as they must when
Orion rises ahead of the sun.

As the sky turns to midnight-blue
I'm watching the hem of peach grow
pale, sensing the lustre of coming days.

And all the cells of my being align,
as if from the pull of a magnet
they start to sway and shimmer.

Holding Firm

i On the Line

I cast my news from Redhead Point
to the honeyeaters on scattered
colour, to the rain churning out

to sea: of a coming birth, a beginning
fresh as the peach blush at the edge
of a day, and there she is – I dream

my mother's mother in her blue dress
faded from the years passed. She bends
above the swelling watery cradle,

claims her line to the unseen soul,
the huddle of snug spirit to come among
the billions, all breathing and beating,

to her great-great-grandchild.
And just now, a butterfly lands
on slender leaves in the foreshore.

ii Early Noting

A song curves beneath the trees in Belmont,
its melody draws her lips to a circle, billows
her lungs, frees her sweet note into the room.

Only three months old, her eyes clear. I wish
for her ears, a list for a lifetime: years of Bach
to Arvo Pärt. And sometime for Beethoven's

Joy rimming the roof of the Concert Hall,
for solo cello, 'Kakadu' and a little Kats-Chernin
with the evening meal, pianissimo.

iii In a Tent

Today I put up the tent, laid
the old green cotton rug inside,
opened the vents to the wind,

invited her in, my grand child,
for stories of the bear called
Corduroy. Most of the time

she rolls around looking out
each netted space on the wispy
repetitions of cloud, the dark

density of tethered leaves,
the wandering swallowtail,
and a flash of slender parrot

through the green garden.
She lives the way I want to
still, heart light, smile wide.

As if in a world stripped of any
genes for war, modified for
love, life and the earth.

iv Sand Leanings

i

That time she found a shell
in the sand, I watched as her finger
touched its cusp and traced

the way along its edge.
She lingered with the lines of dusk
(the lilacs and pinks), then cupped

the bulge in her palm before
she slipped the tip of her finger
over its white inner porcelain.

Just when I thought she was done
she took it to her lips
and licked.

ii

She toddles to the edge of a day
at Caves Beach under the midsummer
moon. Waves fizz clear with foam.

Her fingers grip mine, squeeze against
the shimmery, shivery wet. I lift her high
with each surge and there's her heart

knocking at the wall of her chest.
She shrieks her fear to thrill and back.
And I want the roll and toss and soar

to fill her days, and for her to know
the habits of creatures and clouds
in these Hunter waterways and hills

that shape her still, and I want her
longings quelled by belonging here,
the mother line holding firm.

Notes

For the poem 'Under the Old Tangle', the Osage Orange trees refer to the hedge in Peats Crater in Muogamarra Nature Reserve. The trees were planted in the 1840s before the invention of barbed wire.

With reference to the poem 'Iningai Reserve', the Iningai were the traditional owners who lived along the Thomson River before European settlement. The Iningai Nature Reserve is now part of the Longreach Town Common.

For the poem 'Water Myths', Ludwig Becker was the German artist and naturalist on the Burke and Wills expedition. He died aged 52 in 1861, about two months after he sketched Mutawintji Gorge.

The quote in section iv in the poem 'Greater than the Sum' comes from Ludwig Leichhardt's *Journal of an overland expedition in Australia, from Moreton Bay to Port Essington, a distance of upwards of 3,000 miles, during the years 1844–1845*, sourced from the University of Sydney Library.

Acknowledgements

I want to thank the Australian Society of Authors for the award of a mentorship to work with the poet Brook Emery; Deb Westbury for her guidance during the Strictly Poetry Focus Week at Varuna; and Ron Pretty for his Riversdale poetry workshop. These experiences were pivotal to the writing of this collection.

For their support and encouragement, I am also indebted to the members of the Hunter Writers Centre Poetry Group, the Focus poets, and to others with whom I have discussed my work, in particular to Ruth Cotton, Judy Johnson, Jean Kent, Robin Loftus and Brenda Proudfoot.

*

I am grateful to the editors of the following anthologies and journals in which some of these poems appeared, often with slight changes: *The Cows Have Been There the Whole Time* (Bundanon Poetry Workshop (2008); *famous reporter* 44 (2012); *The Henry Lawson Verse and Short Story Anthology* (2013); *Grieve* (2013, 2014, 2016 and 2017); *Australian Love Poems* (2013); *Once Wild*, Newcastle Poetry Prize (2014); *A Slow Combusting Hymn* (2014); *Watermark*, Hunter Valley Writing (2014); *Home is the Hunter* (2016); *Plumwood Mountain Journal* (2016); *Antipodes* (2016); *The Dangar Island Garbage Boat*, Newcastle Poetry Prize (2016); *Cordite 56.1 EKPHRASTIC* (2016); *Not Very Quiet* Issue 1 (2017) and Issue 2 (2018); and *ear to earth* (2017).

The poems, 'Their Hands' and 'What I admire most about

you, Margaret,' won first and second place respectively in The Henry Lawson Verse and Short Story Competition (2013). 'Under the Old Tangle' and 'A Simple Mix' were long-listed for the Ron Pretty Poetry Prize of 2014 and 2016 respectively. 'Iningai Reserve' was commended in the Toowoomba Writers Festival Literary Prize in 2014 and 'Sydney Rock Orchid' was shortlisted for Royal Botanical Garden, Sydney Poetry Prize in 2016. 'Holding Firm' won the poetry section of the Catchfire Press competition *Home is the Hunter*.

www.ingramcontent.com/pod-product-compliance
Lightning Source LLC
Chambersburg PA
CBHW072207100526
44589CB00015B/2414